A
WOMAN'S
BOOK
OF
INSPIRATION

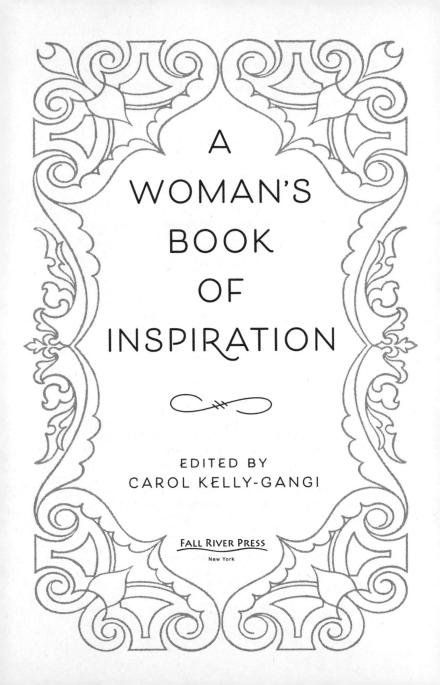

A WOMAN'S BOOK OF INSPIRATION

EDITED BY
CAROL KELLY-GANGI

FALL RIVER PRESS

New York

To all of my sisters with much love,
Barbara, Joanne, Lori, Marianne, Mary, Rose, and Theresa

FALL RIVER PRESS

New York

An Imprint of Sterling Publishing Co., Inc.
1166 Avenue of the Americas
New York, NY 10036

Compilation © 2017 Carol Kelly-Gangi

ISBN 978-1-4351-6647-9

Distributed in Canada by Sterling Publishing Co., Inc.
c/o Canadian Manda Group, 664 Annette Street
Toronto, Ontario M6S 2C8, Canada
Distributed in the United Kingdom by GMC Distribution Services
Castle Place, 166 High Street, Lewes, East Sussex BN7 1XU, England
Distributed in Australia by NewSouth Books
45 Beach Street, Coogee NSW 2034, Australia

For information about custom editions, special sales, and premium
and corporate purchases, please contact Sterling Special Sales at
800-805-5489 or specialsales@sterlingpublishing.com.

Manufactured in the United States of America

6 8 10 9 7

sterlingpublishing.com

CONTENTS

INTRODUCTION

"Nevertheless, she persisted."

During and after the election of 2016, the role of women in society and women's rights took on a new urgency, reflected particularly in a surge of activism and engagement that hasn't been seen in decades. Women young and old are joining forces to speak out on issues ranging from health care to reproductive rights, wage inequality, and transparency in government. But women have been confronting daunting challenges from the dawn of recorded history. What is true then and now is that women persevere. The hundreds of quotations in *A Woman's Book of Inspiration* come from women of all backgrounds and present a fascinating spectrum of ideas, perspectives, and insights.

Of the many universal themes that emerge, there is the love of family; the struggle for freedom, equality, and justice; the quest for knowledge; and the desire for peace and an end to poverty. The quotations themselves, however, are as singular as the women who voiced them. In the excerpts that follow, Virginia Woolf reveals her secret to happiness; Isabel Allende, Melinda Gates, and Sheryl Sandberg speak passionately about empowering women; and Jane Austen, Jane Fonda, Roxane Gay, and Zadie Smith reflect on the true nature of female friendship.

Elsewhere, women reveal some of the profound joys and struggles from their own lives. Harriet Tubman recalls the moment she knew she would die for her freedom. Ruth Bader Ginsburg, Mindy Kaling, and Diane Keaton lovingly recall their mothers; while Tina Fey, Jodie Foster, and Meryl Streep share insights into their own motherhood. Chimamanda Ngozi Adichie, Helen Mirren, and Emma Watson exchange very personal views on feminism; while Angelina Jolie, Hedy Lamarr, Amy Schumer, and Kerry Washington reflect on notions of women and beauty.

In an engaging dialogue that captures a rich array of voices, the contributors also exchange views on such subjects as the meaning of love; the value of education; the art of communication; the world of politics; the role of spirituality; and the meaning of success.

A collection that speaks to not only women, but also to the richness of the human experience, *A Woman's Book of Inspiration* is a testament to women everywhere, past and present, who embody a spirit of strength, determination, nurturing, and hope that is all their own.

—CAROL KELLY-GANGI, 2017

KNOWLEDGE, LEARNING, AND EDUCATION

If you have knowledge, let others light their candles at it.
—MARGARET FULLER

~∽~

I was brought up to believe that the only thing worth doing was to add to the sum of accurate information in the world.
—MARGARET MEAD

Every truth we see is one to give to the world, not to keep to ourselves alone.

—ELIZABETH CADY STANTON

∽∾

We are not what we know but what we are willing to learn.

—MARY CATHERINE BATESON

∽∾

Sit down and read. Educate yourself for the coming conflicts.

—MOTHER JONES

∽∾

My grandfather went to school for one day: to tell the teacher he wouldn't be back. Yet all of his life he read greedily, as did his uneducated friends.

—TONI MORRISON

∽∾

Anybody who has survived his childhood has enough information about life to last him the rest of his days.

—FLANNERY O'CONNOR

∽∾

Home is a child's first and most important classroom.

—HILLARY CLINTON

I am an example of what is possible when girls, from the very beginning of their lives, are loved and nurtured by people around them.

—MICHELLE OBAMA

～✺～

Parents have become so convinced that educators know what is best for children that they forget that they themselves are really experts.

—MARIAN WRIGHT EDELMAN

～✺～

Learning is not attained by chance, it must be sought for with ardor and attended to with diligence.

—ABIGAIL ADAMS

～✺～

Humans are allergic to change. They love to say, "We've always done it this way." I try to fight that. That's why I have a clock on my wall that runs counter-clockwise.

—GRACE HOPPER

～✺～

The first problem for all of us, men and women, is not to learn, but to unlearn.

—GLORIA STEINEM

The most courageous act is still to think for yourself. Aloud.
—Coco Chanel

⌐

The solution to my life occurred to me one evening while I was ironing a shirt.
—Alice Munro

⌐

Trust your hunches. They're usually based on facts filed away just below the conscious level.
—Joyce Brothers

⌐

Think wrongly, if you please, but in all cases think for yourself.
—Doris Lessing

⌐

Prejudices, it is well known, are most difficult to eradicate from the heart whose soil has never been loosened or fertilized by education; they grow there, firm as weeds among rocks.
—Charlotte Brontë

⌐

Part of teaching is helping students learn how to tolerate ambiguity, consider possibilities, and ask questions that are unanswerable.
—Sara Lawrence-Lightfoot

Let us remember: One book, one pen, one child, and one teacher can change the world.

—MALALA YOUSAFZAI

～୨୦～

Schooling is what happens inside the walls of the school, some of which is educational. Education happens everywhere, and it happens from the moment a child is born—and some people say before—until a child dies.

—SARA LAWRENCE-LIGHTFOOT

～୨୦～

I don't know that my schooling was conducive to wild ideas and creativity, but it gave me discipline, drive. They taught me how to think—I really know how to think.

—LADY GAGA

～୨୦～

Education was the most important value in our home when I was growing up. People don't always realize that my parents shared a sense of intellectual curiosity and a love of reading and history.

—CAROLINE KENNEDY

～୨୦～

I'm going to college. I don't care if it ruins my career. I'd rather be smart than a movie star.

—NATALIE PORTMAN

Educate a woman and you educate her family. Educate a girl and you change the future.

—RANIA AL ABDULLAH

Education is the point at which we decide whether we love the world enough to assume responsibility for it, and by the same token save it from that ruin which, except for renewal, except for the coming of the new and young, would be inevitable.

—HANNAH ARENDT

For what is done or learned by one class of women becomes, by virtue of their common womanhood, the property of all women.

—ELIZABETH BLACKWELL

Empower yourselves with a good education, then get out there and use that education to build a country worthy of your boundless promise.

—MICHELLE OBAMA

Love and Friendship

Where there is great love there are
always miracles.

—Willa Cather

⁓

Love is a flower that grows in any soil,
works its sweet miracles undaunted by
autumn frost or winter snow, blooming
fair and fragrant all the year, and blessing
those who give and those who receive.

—Louisa May Alcott

Love makes your soul crawl out from its hiding place.
—Zora Neale Hurston

~ॐ~

How do I love thee? Let me count the ways.
I love thee to the depth and breadth and height
My soul can reach.
—Elizabeth Barrett Browning

~ॐ~

Whatever our souls are made of, his and mine are the same.
—Emily Brontë

~ॐ~

How helpless we are, like netted birds,
when we are caught by desire!
—Belva Plain

~ॐ~

It was enough just to sit there without words.
—Louise Erdrich

Love at first sight is easy to understand; it's when two people have been looking at each other for a lifetime that it becomes a miracle.

—AMY BLOOM

Love is not enough. It must be the foundation, the cornerstone, but not the complete structure. It is much too pliable, too yielding.

—BETTE DAVIS

How did a person survive without intimacy? Didn't you need at least one person in the world to know who you really were?

—JUDITH FREEMAN

If love does not know how to give and take without restrictions, it is not love, but a transaction.

—EMMA GOLDMAN

It's so clear that you have to cherish everyone. I think that's what I get from these older black women, that every soul is to be cherished, that every flower is to bloom.

—ALICE WALKER

Is there any stab as deep as wondering where and how much you
failed those you loved?
—Florida Scott-Maxwell

∽

The most vital right is the right to love and be loved.
—Emma Goldman

∽

When you put love out in the world it travels, and it can touch
people and reach people in ways that we never even expected.
—Laverne Cox

∽

That Love is all there is,
Is all we know of Love.
—Emily Dickinson

∽

Female friendship has been the bedrock of women's lives for as
long as there have been women.
—Rebecca Traister

∽

Friendship with oneself is all important because without it one
cannot be friends with anybody else in the world.
—Eleanor Roosevelt

Each friend represents a world in us,
a world possibly not born until they arrive,
and it is only by this meeting that a new world is born.

—ANAÏS NIN

Women understand. We may share experiences, make jokes,
paint pictures, and describe humiliations that mean little to men,
but women understand.

—GLORIA STEINEM

I felt it shelter to speak to you.

—EMILY DICKINSON

Some people go to priests; others to poetry; I to my friends.

—VIRGINIA WOOLF

Friendship is the finest balm for the pangs of despised love.

—JANE AUSTEN

What I cannot love, I overlook. Is that real friendship?

—ANAÏS NIN

There is nothing I would not do for those who are really my friends. I have no notion of loving people by halves; it is not my nature.

—JANE AUSTEN

⌒

It's easy to be friends when everyone's 18. It gets harder the older you get, as you make different life choices, as people say in America. A lot of women's friendships begin to founder. I was interested in why that was, why it's not possible for a woman to see her friend living differently and just think, "Oh, she lives differently."

—ZADIE SMITH

⌒

Abandon the cultural myth that all female friendships must be bitchy, toxic or competitive. This myth is like heels and purses—pretty but designed to slow women down.

—ROXANE GAY

⌒

A breakup with a female friend can be more traumatic than a breakup with a lover.

—KEIRA KNIGHTLEY

I think that is one reason why women live longer than men. Friendship between women is different than friendship between men. We talk about different things. We delve deep. . . . It's my women friends that keep starch in my spine and without them, I don't know where I would be.

—JANE FONDA

∽

There's a kind of emotional exploration you plumb with a friend that you don't really do with your family.

—BETTE MIDLER

∽

I love my husband, but it is nothing like a conversation with a woman that understands you.

—BEYONCÉ

∽

The growth of true friendship may be a lifelong affair.

—SARAH ORNE JEWETT

Happiness, Fulfillment, and Life's Pleasures

There is only one happiness in life,
to love and be loved.
—George Sand

~∞~

It's only possible to live happily ever after
on a day to day basis.
—Margaret Bonnano

Happiness is not a matter of events;
it depends upon the tides of the mind.

—Alice Meynell

～⚬～

But I don't think of the future, or the past, I feast on the moment.
This is the secret of happiness, but only reached now in middle age.

—Virginia Woolf

～⚬～

I have learned from experience that the greater part of our
happiness or misery depends on our dispositions
and not on our circumstances.

—Martha Washington

～⚬～

Life appears to me to be too short to be spent in nursing
animosity or registering wrong.

—Charlotte Brontë

～⚬～

Happiness is not a goal; it is a by-product.

—Eleanor Roosevelt

～⚬～

It is the ultimate luxury to combine passion and contribution.
It's also a very clear path to happiness.

—Sheryl Sandberg

Personal happiness lies in knowing that life is not a checklist of acquisition or achievement. Your qualifications … are not your life.

—J.K. Rowling

⌒

Happiness is a matter of one's most ordinary and everyday mode of consciousness being busy and lively and unconcerned with self.

—Iris Murdoch

⌒

Happiness is good health and a bad memory.

—Ingrid Bergman

⌒

When one door of happiness closes, another opens; but often we look so long at the closed door that we do not see the one which has been opened for us.

—Helen Keller

⌒

If only we'd stop trying to be happy we could have a pretty good time.

—Edith Wharton

⌒

One half of the world cannot understand the pleasures of the other.

—Jane Austen

Eden is that old-fashioned house
We dwell in every day
Without suspecting our abode
Until we drive away.

—Emily Dickinson

～∘～

Many persons have a wrong idea of what constitutes happiness.
It is not attained through self-gratification but through fidelity
to a worthy purpose.

—Helen Keller

～∘～

When so rich a harvest is before us, why do we not gather it?
All is in our hands if we will but use it.

—St. Elizabeth Ann Seton

～∘～

Why not seize the pleasure at once? How often is happiness
destroyed by preparation, foolish preparation!

—Jane Austen

～∘～

Everyone has inside of her a piece of good news. The good news
is that you don't know how great you can be! How much you can
love! What you can accomplish! And what your potential is!

—Anne Frank

I'm afraid I'm an incorrigible life-lover, life-wonderer,
and adventurer.
—EDITH WHARTON

⌁

Laughter by definition is healthy.
—DORIS LESSING

⌁

The best remedy for those who are afraid, lonely or unhappy is
to go outside, somewhere where they can be quiet, alone with the
heavens, nature, and God. Because only then does one feel that all
is as it should be and that God wishes to see people happy,
amidst the simple beauty of nature.
—ANNE FRANK

⌁

I think I should have no other mortal wants, if I could always have
plenty of music. It seems to infuse strength into my limbs, and
ideas into my brain. Life seems to go on without effort,
when I am filled with music.
—GEORGE ELIOT

⌁

A house is no home unless it contains food and fire for the mind
as well as for the body.
—MARGARET FULLER

Just the knowledge that a good book is waiting one at the end of a
long day makes that day happier.

—Kathleen Norris

⁓∽⁓

Please, no matter how we advance technologically, please don't
abandon the book. There is nothing in our material world more
beautiful than the book.

—Patti Smith

⁓∽⁓

In books I have traveled, not only to other worlds,
but into my own.

—Anna Quindlen

⁓∽⁓

Poetry, I have discovered, is always unexpected and always as
faithful and honest as dreams.

—Alice Walker

⁓∽⁓

God comes to us in theater in the way we communicate with each
other, whether it be a symphony orchestra, or a wonderful ballet,
or a beautiful painting, or a play.
It's a way of expressing our humanity.

—Julie Harris

The dancer's body is simply the luminous
manifestation of the soul.

—ISADORA DUNCAN

꘎

Somewhere behind the athlete you've become and the hours of
practice and the coaches who have pushed you is a little girl who
fell in love with the game and never looked back … play for her.

—MIA HAMM

꘎

The game of baseball has always been linked in my mind with the
mystic texture of childhood, with the sounds and smells of summer
nights and with the memories of my father.

—DORIS KEARNS GOODWIN

꘎

Cooking is like love. It should be entered into
with abandon or not at all.

—HARRIET VAN HORNE

꘎

To travel is worth any cost or sacrifice.

—ELIZABETH GILBERT

What a wonderful life I've had! I only wish I'd realized it sooner.

—Colette

～⌘～

Seize the moment. Remember all those women on the *Titanic*
who waved off the dessert cart.

—Erma Bombeck

～⌘～

If you obey all the rules, you miss all the fun.

—Katharine Hepburn

～⌘～

I finally figured out the only reason to be alive is to enjoy it.

—Rita Mae Brown

～⌘～

To love what you do and feel that it matters—
how could anything be more fun?

—Katharine Graham

Marriage, Children, and Family

Happiness in marriage is entirely
a matter of chance.

—Jane Austen

∼ೋ∼

The first great step is to like yourself
enough to pick someone who likes you, too.

—Jane O'Reilly

Domestic peace! best joy of earth.
When shall we all thy value learn?
—Anne Brontë

~⌇~

That quiet mutual gaze of a trusting husband and wife
is like the first moment of rest or refuge
from a great weariness or a great danger.
—George Eliot

~⌇~

When I'm weak, you can be strong; when I'm strong,
you can be weak. That's what I believe marriage is.
—Gisele Bundchen

~⌇~

If you have a caring life partner, you help the other person when
that person needs it. I had a life partner who thought my work was
as important as his, and I think that made all the difference for me.
—Ruth Bader Ginsburg

~⌇~

A successful marriage requires falling in love many times,
always with the same person.
—Mignon McLaughlin

Sexiness wears thin after a while and beauty fades, but to be
married to a man who makes you laugh every day,
ah, now that's a real treat.

—Joanne Woodward

⮾

Wasn't marriage, like life, unstimulating and unprofitable
and somewhat empty when too well ordered and protected and
guarded. Wasn't it finer, more splendid, more nourishing,
when it was, like life itself, a mixture of the sordid and the
magnificent; of mud and stars; of earth and flowers;
of love and hate and laughter and tears and ugliness
and beauty and hurt?

—Edna Ferber

⮾

If you want to sacrifice the admiration of many men for the
criticism of one, go ahead, get married.

—Katharine Hepburn

⮾

I love being married. It's so great to find that one special person
you want to annoy for the rest of your life.

—Rita Rudner

Why does a woman work ten years to change a man's habits and then complain that he's not the man she married?

—Barbra Streisand

~∞~

Once a woman has forgiven her man,
she must not reheat his sins for breakfast.

—Marlene Dietrich

~∞~

One of the trials of woman-kind is the fear of being an old maid. To escape this dreadful doom, young girls rush into matrimony with a recklessness which astonishes the beholder; never pausing to remember that the loss of liberty, happiness, and self-respect is poorly repaid by the barren honor of being called "Mrs." instead of "Miss."

—Louisa May Alcott

~∞~

I don't think that because I'm not married it's made my life any less. That old maid myth is garbage.

—Diane Keaton

~∞~

Scratch a lover, and find a foe.

—Dorothy Parker

A divorce is like an amputation. You survive,
but there's less of you.
—MARGARET ATWOOD

~·~

I do not consider divorce an evil by any means. It is just as much
a refuge for women married to brutal men as Canada was to the
slaves of brutal masters.
—SUSAN B. ANTHONY

~·~

When a marriage ends, who is left to understand it?
—JOYCE CAROL OATES

~·~

Making the decision to have a child—it's momentous.
It is to decide forever to have your heart go walking around
outside your body.
—ELIZABETH STONE

~·~

Bringing a child into the world is the greatest act of hope there is.
—LOUISE HART

Why had no one told me that my body would become a battlefield, a sacrifice, a test? Why did I not know that birth is the pinnacle where women discover the courage to become mothers?

—ANITA DIAMANT

Being a mom has made me so tired. And so happy.

—TINA FEY

Though motherhood is the most important of all professions— requiring more knowledge than any other department in human affairs—there was no attention given to preparation for this office.

—ELIZABETH CADY STANTON

When you are a mother, you are never really alone in your thoughts. A mother always has to think twice, once for herself and once for her child.

—SOPHIA LOREN

A mother's love for her child is like nothing else in the world. It knows no law, no pity, it dares all things and crushes down remorselessly all that stands in its path.

—AGATHA CHRISTIE

Mothers are the most instinctive philosophers.
—HARRIET BEECHER STOWE

~

Motherhood has a very humanizing effect. Everything gets
reduced to essentials.
—MERYL STREEP

~

Even when you plan to have a family, you never know who the
person is going to be that you decide to become a parent to.
We're accidentally born to our own parents.
—LOUISE ERDRICH

~

Love and respect are the most important aspects of parenting,
and of all relationships.
—JODIE FOSTER

~

A child is fed with milk and praise.
—MARY LAMB

You really do need a parent who's willing to set themselves aside,
and their own hopes and dreams. If your child marches
to a different beat, a different drummer, you might just have
to go along with that music. Help them achieve what's
important to them.

—SONIA SOTOMAYOR

Who would ever think here that so much can go on in the soul
of a young girl?

—ANNE FRANK

Children require guidance and sympathy
far more than instruction.

—ANNE SULLIVAN

Mummy herself has told us that she looked upon us more as
her friends than her daughters. Now that is all very fine, but still, a
friend can't take a mother's place.

—ANNE FRANK

If you bungle raising your children, I don't think whatever else you do well matters very much.

—JACQUELINE KENNEDY ONASSIS

~⌒~

My relationship with my mom is really the single most profound relationship that I've ever had in my life.

—MINDY KALING

~⌒~

My mother was really my partner in every project that I had. She was just the great enabler of my dreams.

—DIANE KEATON

~⌒~

I have a last thank-you. It is to my mother Celia Amster Bader, the bravest and strongest person I have known, who was taken from me much too soon. I pray that I may be all that she would have been had she lived in an age when women could aspire and achieve and daughters are cherished as much as sons.

—RUTH BADER GINSBURG, ON ACCEPTING HER NOMINATION TO THE U.S.
SUPREME COURT, JUNE 14, 1993

~⌒~

No matter how old a mother is, she watches her middle-aged children for signs of improvement.

—FLORIDA SCOTT-MAXWELL

By and large, mothers and housewives are the only workers
who do not have regular time off.
They are the great vacationless class.
—Anne Morrow Lindbergh

Few tasks are more like the torture of Sisyphus than housework,
with its endless repetition: The clean becomes soiled, the soiled is
made clean, over and over, day after day.
—Simone de Beauvoir

When men reach their sixties and retire, they go to pieces.
Women go right on cooking.
—Gail Sheehy

Sister is probably the most competitive relationship within the
family, but once the sisters are grown, it becomes the strongest
relationship.
—Margaret Mead

I think a dysfunctional family is any family with
more than one person in it.
—Mary Karr

Family life! The United Nations is child's play compared to the tugs and splits and need to understand and forgive in any family.

—MAY SARTON

∽

The great advantage of living in a large family is that early lesson of life's essential unfairness.

—NANCY MITFORD

∽

One of the oldest human needs is having someone to wonder where you are when you don't come home at night.

—MARGARET MEAD

∽

We are linked by blood, and blood is memory without language.

—JOYCE CAROL OATES

Life's
Obstacles

*I was taught that the way of progress is
neither swift nor easy.*
—Marie Curie

~⁓~

*We could never learn to be brave and
patient, if there were only joy in the world.*
—Helen Keller

When you get into a tight place and it seems you can't go on,
hold on, for that's just the place and the time that the
tide will turn.

—Harriet Beecher Stowe

∼⌒∼

If you have made mistakes, even serious ones, there is always
another chance for you. What we call failure is not the falling
down, but the staying down.

—Mary Pickford

∼⌒∼

It is impossible to live without failing at something, unless you
live so cautiously that you might as well not have lived at all—
in which case, you fail by default.

—J.K. Rowling

∼⌒∼

There are no mistakes, no coincidences. All events are
blessings given to us to learn from.

—Elizabeth Kubler-Ross

∼⌒∼

I learned compassion from being discriminated against.
Everything bad that's ever happened to me has taught
me compassion.

—Ellen DeGeneres

Please know that I am aware of the hazards. I want to do it because I want to do it. Women must try to do things as men have tried. When they fail, their failure must be but a challenge to others.

—Amelia Earhart

～∽～

I didn't have anybody, really, no foundation in life, so I had to make my own way. Always, from the start. I had to go out in the world and become strong, to discover my mission in life.

—Tina Turner

～∽～

A depressing and difficult passage has prefaced every new page I have turned in life.

—Charlotte Brontë

～∽～

When you're 50, you start thinking about things you haven't thought about before. I used to think getting old was about vanity, but actually it's about losing people you love.
Getting wrinkles is trivial.

—Joyce Carol Oates

～∽～

Illness is the night-side of life, a more onerous citizenship. Everyone who is born holds dual citizenship, in the kingdom of the well and in the kingdom of the sick.

—Susan Sontag

I did not lose myself all at once. I rubbed out my face over the years washing away my pain, the same way carvings on stone are worn down by water.

—AMY TAN

~

I would like to learn, or remember, how to live.

—ANNIE DILLARD

~

Showing up for life. Being blessed with the rebirth that recovery brings.
One day at a time.

—BETTY FORD

~

Great events make me quiet and calm; it is only trifles that irritate my nerves.

—QUEEN VICTORIA

~

Worry does not empty tomorrow of its sorrow. It empties today of its strength.

—CORRIE TEN BOOM

We must accept our pain, change what we can,
and laugh at the rest.

—CAMILLE PAGLIA

~~

We never know how high we are
'Til we are called to rise;
And then, if we are true to plan,
Our statures touch the skies.

—EMILY DICKINSON

~~

I like living. I have sometimes been wildly, despairingly, acutely
miserable, racked with sorrow, but through it all I still know quite
certainly that just to be alive is a grand thing.

—AGATHA CHRISTIE

FREEDOM, EQUALITY, AND JUSTICE

The right to vote, or equal civil rights, may be good demands, but true emancipation begins neither at the polls nor in courts. It begins in woman's soul.

—EMMA GOLDMAN

~§~

Those men and women are fortunate who are born at a time when a great struggle for human freedom is in progress.

—EMMELINE PANKHURST

The political core of any movement for freedom in the society has
to have the political imperative to protect free speech.

—BELL HOOKS

⁓

We realize the importance of our voices
only when they are silenced.

—MALALA YOUSAFZAI

⁓

Freedom is the very essence of our economy and society.
Without freedom the human mind is prevented from unleashing
its creative force. But what is also clear is that this freedom
does not stand alone. It is freedom in responsibility and
freedom to exercise responsibility.

—ANGELA MERKEL

⁓

Liberty, taking the word in its concrete sense,
consists in the ability to choose.

—SIMONE WEIL

⁓

None who have always been free can understand the terrible
fascinating power of the hope of freedom to those who are not free.

—PEARL S. BUCK

I had reasoned this out in my mind, there were two things I had a right to: liberty and death. If I could not have one, I would have the other, for no man should take me alive.

—HARRIET TUBMAN

Freedom is fragile and must be protected. To sacrifice it, even as a temporary measure, is to betray it.

—GERMAINE GREER

Struggle is a never ending process. Freedom is never really won you earn it and win it in every generation.

—CORETTA SCOTT KING

We have only one real shot at liberation, and that is to emancipate ourselves from within.

—COLETTE DOWLING

Do not put such unlimited power into the hands of the Husbands. Remember all Men would be tyrants if they could. If particular care and attention is not paid to the Ladies, we are determined to foment a Rebellion, and will not hold ourselves bound by any Laws in which we have no voice, or Representation.

—ABIGAIL ADAMS, LETTER TO HER HUSBAND, JOHN ADAMS, MARCH 31, 1776

The day will come when man will recognize woman as his peer,
not only at the fireside, but in councils of the nation.
Then, and not until then, will there be the perfect comradeship,
the ideal union between the sexes that shall result in the highest
development of the race.

—SUSAN B. ANTHONY

I have ploughed, and planted, and gathered into barns, and no
man could head me! And ain't I a woman? I could work as much
and eat as much as a man—when I could get it—and bear the lash
as well! And ain't I a woman?

—SOJOURNER TRUTH

I am not free while any woman is unfree, even when her shackles
are very different from my own.

—AUDRE LORDE

I am glad to see that men are getting their rights,
but I want women to get theirs, and while the water is stirring
I will step into the pool.

—SOJOURNER TRUTH

I declare to you that woman must not depend upon
the protection of man, but must be taught to protect herself and
there I take my stand.

—SUSAN B. ANTHONY

If society will not admit of woman's free development, then
society must be remodeled.

—ELIZABETH BLACKWELL

"Organize, agitate, educate," must be our war cry.

—SUSAN B. ANTHONY

There is no female mind. The brain is not an organ of sex. Might
as well speak of a female liver.

—CHARLOTTE PERKINS GILMAN

I am neither a man nor a woman but an author.

—CHARLOTTE BRONTË

You have to be taught to be second class; you're not born that way.

—LENA HORNE

If we are to achieve a richer culture, rich in contrasting values, we must recognize the whole gamut of human potentialities, and so weave a less arbitrary social fabric, one in which each diverse human gift will find a fitting place.

—MARGARET MEAD

No one can make you feel inferior without your consent.

—ELEANOR ROOSEVELT

I had felt for a long time, that if I was ever told to get up so a white person could sit, that I would refuse to do so.

—ROSA PARKS

We first crush people to the earth, and then claim the right of trampling upon them because they are prostrate.

—LYDIA MARIA CHILD

We should not be held back from pursuing our full talents, from contributing what we could contribute to the society, because we fit into a certain mold—because we belong to a group that historically has been the object of discrimination.

—RUTH BADER GINSBURG

I've run into more discrimination as a woman
than as an Indian.

—WILMA PEARL MANKILLER

∼⚬∼

Of my two "handicaps," being female put many more obstacles
in my path than being black.

—SHIRLEY CHISHOLM

∼⚬∼

As long as you keep a person down, some part of you has to be
down there to hold him down, so it means you cannot
soar as you otherwise might.

—MARIAN ANDERSON

∼⚬∼

The time is at hand when the voices of the feminine mystique can
no longer drown out the inner voice that is driving women
on to become complete.

—BETTY FRIEDAN

∼⚬∼

My idea of feminism is self-determination, and it's very
open-ended; every woman has the right to become herself,
and do whatever she needs to do.

—ANI DIFRANCO

I myself have never been able to find out precisely what feminism is. I only know that people call me a feminist whenever I express sentiments that differentiate me from a doormat or a prostitute.

—REBECCA WEST

⁓

"I hate discussions of feminism that end up with who does the dishes," she said. So do I. But at the end, there are always the damned dishes.

—MARILYN FRENCH

⁓

Some of us are becoming the men we wanted to marry.

—GLORIA STEINEM

⁓

In my heart, I think a woman has two choices: Either she's a feminist or a masochist.

—GLORIA STEINEM

⁓

To me, a feminist belongs in the same category as a humanist or an advocate for human rights. I don't see why someone who's a feminist should be thought of differently.

—SUZANNE VEGA

No matter what sex you are, or race, be a feminist. In every country and culture that I have visited, from Sweden to Uganda, from Singapore to Mali, it is clear that when women are given respect, and the ability and freedom to pursue their personal dreams and ambitions, life improves for everyone.

—HELEN MIRREN

Feminist politics aims to end domination,
to free us to be who we are—
to live lives where we love justice,
where we can live in peace.
Feminism is for everybody.

—BELL HOOKS

We want to try to galvanize as many men and boys as possible to be advocates for change.

—EMMA WATSON

Does feminist mean large unpleasant person who'll shout at you, or someone who believes women are human beings? To me, it's the latter, so I sign up.

—MARGARET ATWOOD

My own definition of a feminist is a man or a woman who says, "Yes, there's a problem with gender as it is today and we must fix it, we must do better."
—Chimamanda Ngozi Adichie

⁓

Women will have achieved true equality when men share with them the responsibility of bringing up the next generation.
—Ruth Bader Ginsburg

⁓

I am a candidate for the Presidency of the United States. I make that statement proudly, in the full knowledge that, as a black person and as a female person, I do not have a chance of actually gaining that office in this election year.
—Shirley Chisholm

⁓

We've chosen the path to equality; don't let them turn us around.
—Geraldine A. Ferraro

I especially treasure the young women who say that my example has inspired them to raise their sights so that they now feel that serving as secretary of state or in even higher office is a realistic goal.

—Madeleine Albright

~~

A little girl grows up in Jim Crow Birmingham and she becomes the secretary of state.

—Condoleezza Rice

~~

I wake up every morning in a house that was built by slaves. And I watch my daughters, two beautiful, intelligent, black young women playing with their dogs on the White House lawn.

—Michelle Obama

~~

To all the little girls who are watching, never doubt that you are valuable and powerful and deserving of every chance and opportunity in the world to pursue and achieve your own dreams.

—Hillary Clinton

Somewhere out in this audience may even be someone who will one day follow in my footsteps, and preside over the White House as the President's spouse. I wish him well!

—BARBARA BUSH

⁓ↄ⁓

We are in the midst of a violent backlash against feminism.

—NAOMI WOLF

⁓ↄ⁓

Real change will come when powerful women are less of an exception. It is easy to dislike senior women because there are so few.

—SHERYL SANDBERG

⁓ↄ⁓

Today there are people trying to take away rights that our mothers, grandmothers and great-grandmothers fought for: our right to vote, our right to choose, affordable quality education, equal pay, access to health care. We the people can't let that happen.

—KERRY WASHINGTON

⁓ↄ⁓

It is past time for women to take their rightful place, side by side with men, in the rooms where the fates of peoples, where their children's and grandchildren's fates, are decided.

—HILLARY CLINTON

My address is like my shoes. It travels with me.
I abide where there is a fight against wrong.

—MOTHER JONES

～

Social change rarely comes about through the efforts of the
disenfranchised. The middle class creates social revolutions.
When a group of people are disproportionately concerned with
daily survival, it's not likely that they have the resources to go to
Washington and march.

—FAYE WATTLETON

～

The first resistance to social change is to say it's not necessary.

—GLORIA STEINEM

～

For all the injustices in our past and our present, we have to
believe that in the free exchange of ideas, justice will prevail over
injustice, tolerance over intolerance and progress over reaction.

—HILLARY CLINTON

～

The struggle is eternal. The tribe increases.
Somebody else carries on.

—ELLA J. BAKER

Government, Politics, War, and Peace

Government is not some make believe
thing that has an independent will of
its own. In our democracy, government is
just how we describe all of the things that
"we the people" have already decided to
do together.

—Elizabeth Warren

～

Men alone are not capable of making laws
for men and women.

—Nellie McClung

There cannot be true democracy unless women's voices are heard.
There cannot be true democracy unless women are given the
opportunity to take responsibility for their own lives.
There cannot be true democracy unless all citizens are able to
participate fully in the lives of their country.

—Hillary Clinton

❧

You can't have a Congress that responds to the needs
of the workingman when there are practically no people here
who represent him. And you're not going to have a society
that understands its humanity if you don't have more women
in government.

—Bella Abzug

❧

If American politics are too dirty for women to take part in,
there's something wrong with American politics.

—Edna Ferber

❧

Truthfulness has never been counted among the political
virtues, and lies have always been regarded as justifiable tools
in political dealings.

—Hannah Arendt

If you want to push something in politics you're accused of being aggressive, and that's not supposed to be a good thing for a woman. If you get upset and show it, you're accused of being emotional.

—MARY HARNEY

The word's out: I'm a woman, and I'm going to have trouble backing off on that. I am what I am. I'll go out and talk to people about what's happening to their families, and when I do that, I'm a mother. I'm a grandmother.

—ELIZABETH WARREN

The first woman President will have to show that she has all of the marbles required to run the government on her own.

—DIANNE FEINSTEIN

We have made tremendous strides since 1920. Women have a stronger voice in our communities and in our workplace. I am proud to serve as one of the 14 women, Republican and Democrat, in the United States Senate, and now we have 62 women in the House of Representatives. We have made progress, but much more needs to be done.

—BARBARA BOXER, IN A LETTER ON THE ANNIVERSARY OF THE RATIFICATION OF THE 19TH AMENDMENT, AUGUST 18, 2003

I hope that young people will also look to politics as a vehicle to not only have their voices heard, but actually to be the change makers that they want to see.

—CHELSEA CLINTON

The politicians were talking themselves red, white, and blue in the face.

—CLARE BOOTH LUCE

The problem is, of course, that these interest groups are all asking for changes, but their enthusiasm for change rapidly disappears when it affects the core of their own interests.

—ANGELA MERKEL

I'm also very proud to be a liberal. Why is that so terrible these days? The liberals were liberating. They fought slavery, fought for women to have the right to vote ... fought to end segregation, fought to end apartheid. Thanks to the liberals, we have Social Security, public education, consumer and environmental protection, Medicare, Medicaid, the minimum-wage law, unemployment compensation. Liberals put an end to child labor. They even gave us the five-day work week. What's to be ashamed of?

—BARBRA STREISAND

I always cheer up immensely if an attack is particularly wounding because I think, well, if they attack one personally, it means they have not a single political argument left.

—MARGARET THATCHER

⸻

The first Republican I knew was my father and he is still the Republican I most admire. He joined our party because the Democrats in Jim Crow Alabama of 1952 would not register him to vote. The Republicans did. My father has never forgotten that day, and neither have I.

—CONDOLEEZZA RICE

⸻

Americans are fighters. We're tough, resourceful and creative, and if we have the chance to fight on a level playing field, where everyone pays a fair share and everyone has a real shot, then no one—no one can stop us.

—ELIZABETH WARREN

⸻

I stand at the altar of the murdered men, and while I live, I fight their cause.

—FLORENCE NIGHTINGALE

You can no more win a war than you can win an earthquake.

—Jeanette Rankin

~

Women more than men can strip war of its glamour and its out-of-date heroisms and patriotisms, and see it as a demon of destruction and hideous wrong.

—Lillian Wald

~

Women have always been the primary victims of war. Women lose their husbands, their fathers, their sons in combat.

—Hillary Clinton

~

We've been a country that's been fortunate to be protected by two oceans, to not have serious attacks on our territory for most of our history. And we were unfortunately reminded in a very devastating way of our vulnerability.

—Condoleezza Rice

~

A leader who doesn't hesitate before he sends his nation into battle is not fit to be a leader.

—Golda Meir

That is what leadership is all about: staking your ground ahead of where opinion is and convincing people, not simply following the popular opinion of the moment.

—DORIS KEARNS GOODWIN

In the future, there will be no female leaders.
There will just be leaders.

—SHERYL SANDBERG

The only alternative to war is peace and the only road to peace is negotiations.

—GOLDA MEIR

For it isn't enough to talk about peace. One must believe in it.
And it isn't enough to believe in it. One must work at it.

—ELEANOR ROOSEVELT

It is absolutely no accident that the peace and reconciliation, and indeed the economic progress, that eluded us generation after generation for hundreds of years, has at last come to pass in an Ireland where the talents of women are now flooding every aspect of life as never before.

—MARY MCALEESE

Women are fifty-one percent of humankind. Empowering them will change everything. I can promise you that. Women working together, linked, informed and educated can bring peace and prosperity to this forsaken land.

—Isabel Allende

~୨୧~

Especially now when views are becoming more polarized, we must work to understand each other across political, religious and national boundaries.

—Jane Goodall

~୨୧~

You can't shake hands with a clenched fist.

—Indira Gandhi

~୨୧~

Every act of love is a work of peace, no matter how small.

—Mother Teresa

WORK, SUCCESS, AND FAME

I believe in hard work. It keeps the wrinkles out of the mind and the spirit.

—HELENA RUBINSTEIN

~∞~

We must believe in ourselves or no one else will believe in us; we must match our aspirations with the competence, courage and determination to succeed.

—ROSALYN YALOW

I have had an incredible journey full of unexpected surprises and daring-do, whether braving my own kitchen to produce a decent meal for my son or tracking down Egypt's Hosni Mubarak in the dying days of his regime.

—CHRISTIANE AMANPOUR

In twenty years I've never had a day when I didn't have to think about someone else's needs. And this means the writing has to be fitted around it.

—ALICE MUNRO

Across the curve of the earth, there are women getting up before dawn, in the blackness before the point of light, in the twilight before sunrise; there are women rising earlier than men and children to break the ice, to start the stove, to put up the pap, the coffee, the rice, to iron the pants, to braid the hair, to pull the day's water up from the well, to boil water for tea, to wash the children for school, to pull the vegetables and start the walk to market, to run to catch the bus for the work that is paid.
I don't know when most women sleep.

—ADRIENNE RICH

When I see the elaborate study and ingenuity displayed by women in the pursuit of trifles, I feel no doubt of their capacity for the most herculean undertakings.

—Julia Ward Howe

~⚬~

God gives talent. Work transforms talent into genius.

—Anna Pavlova

~⚬~

Find something you're passionate about and keep tremendously interested in it.

—Julia Child

~⚬~

Never work just for money or for power. They won't save your soul or help you sleep at night.

—Marian Wright Edelman

~⚬~

A woman will always have to be better than a man in any job she undertakes.

—Eleanor Roosevelt

The thing women have yet to learn is nobody gives you power.
You just take it.

—ROSEANNE BARR

∽∾

What is sad for women of my generation is that they weren't
supposed to work if they had families. What were they going to do
when the children are grown—watch the raindrops coming down
the window pane?

—JACQUELINE KENNEDY ONASSIS

∽∾

But the problem is that when I go around and speak on campuses,
I still don't get young men standing up and saying, "How can I
combine career and family?"

—GLORIA STEINEM

∽∾

At work, you think of the children you have left at home. At
home, you think of the work you've left unfinished. Such a struggle
is unleashed within yourself. Your heart is rent.

—GOLDA MEIR

∽∾

You tell me who has to leave the office when the kid bumps his
head or slips on a milk carton.

—WENDY WASSERSTEIN

Careers are a jungle gym, not a ladder.
—SHERYL SANDBERG

I don't believe in careers. I believe in work.
—DEBRA WINGER

I just love bossy women. I could be around them all day. To me, bossy is not a pejorative term at all. It means somebody's passionate and engaged and ambitious and doesn't mind leading.
—AMY POEHLER

Opportunities are usually disguised as hard work, so most people don't recognize them.
—ANN LANDERS

It is shameful that there are so few women in science.... There is a misconception in America that women scientists are all dowdy spinsters. This is the fault of men.
—CHIEN-SHIUNG WU

My love affair with the brain started when I was a child growing up in the country. At night, I would look at the stars and wonder where the sky ended.

—MARIAN C. DIAMOND

When you cease to make a contribution, you begin to die.

—ELEANOR ROOSEVELT

Laziness may appear attractive, but work gives satisfaction.

—ANNE FRANK

I've never sought success in order to get fame and money; it's the talent and the passion that count in success.

—INGRID BERGMAN

Success can make you go one of two ways. It can make you a prima donna, or it can smooth the edges, take away the insecurities, let the nice things come out.

—BARBARA WALTERS

You can't get spoiled if you do your own ironing.

—MERYL STREEP

Women who are confident of their abilities are more likely to succeed than those who lack confidence, even though the latter may be much more competent and talented and industrious.

—Joyce Brothers

⁓

I've always believed that one woman's success can only help another woman's success.

—Gloria Vanderbilt

⁓

It is better to be young in your failures than old in your successes.

—Flannery O'Connor

⁓

The penalty of success is to be bored by people who used to snub you.

—Lady Nancy Astor

⁓

There is no point at which you can say, 'Well, I'm successful now. I might as well take a nap.'

—Carrie Fisher

⁓

The secret of joy in work is contained in one word—excellence. To know how to do something well is to enjoy it.

—Pearl S. Buck

When you perform . . . you are out of yourself—larger and more potent, more beautiful. You are for minutes heroic. This is power. This is glory on earth. And it is yours, nightly.

—AGNES DE MILLE

~

When I'm performing I'm not afraid of anything or anybody. But when I'm just me I have this fright of being a disappointment to the people.

—BARBRA STREISAND

~

I restore myself when I'm alone. A career is born in public— talent in privacy.

—MARILYN MONROE

~

You really can't function as a celebrity. Entertainers are celebrities. I'm an architect. I'm an artist. I make things.

—MAYA LIN

~

Fame lost its appeal for me when I went into a public restroom and an autograph seeker handed me a pen and paper under the stall door.

—MARLO THOMAS

The best fame is a writer's fame: it's enough to get a table at a good restaurant, but not enough that you get interrupted when you eat.

—FRAN LEBOWITZ

I want to be known as an actress. I'm not royalty.

—ELIZABETH TAYLOR

Celebrity is the religion of our time.

—MAUREEN DOWD

If you survive long enough, you're revered—
rather like an old building.

—KATHARINE HEPBURN

I am independent! I can live alone and I love to work.

—MARY CASSATT

Work is and always has been my salvation
and I thank the Lord for it.

—LOUISA MAY ALCOTT

Women
and Beauty

When you are balanced and when you listen and attend to the needs of your body, mind, and spirit, your natural beauty comes out.

—Christy Turlington

∼∽

Any girl can be glamorous; all you have to do is stand still and look stupid.

—Hedy Lamarr

My beauty is not about how I look.
My beauty is about my heart and soul.

—LAVERNE COX

❧

The girls who were unanimously considered beautiful often rested
on their beauty alone. I felt I had to do things, to be intelligent
and develop a personality in order to be seen as attractive.
By the time I realized maybe I wasn't plain and might even
possibly be pretty, I had already trained myself to be a little more
interesting and informed.

—DIANE VON FURSTENBERG

❧

Barefoot or first thing in the morning, I feel beautiful. I didn't
always feel that way, but I feel that way now. When somebody loves
you, and when you make somebody else happy, when your
presence seems to make them happy, you suddenly feel like the
most beautiful person in the world.

—ANGELINA JOLIE

❧

Brains are an asset—if you hide them.

—MAE WEST

❧

There's no better makeup than self-confidence.

—SHAKIRA

The fact of the matter is that you can use your beauty and use your charm and be flirtatious, and you can get people interested in your beauty. But you cannot maintain that. In the end, talent is the only thing. My work is the only thing that's going to change any minds.

—MADONNA

Let me tell you something—being thought of as a beautiful woman has spared me nothing in life. No heartache, no trouble. Love has been difficult. Beauty is essentially meaningless and it is always transitory.

—HALLE BERRY

Character contributes to beauty. It fortifies a woman as her youth fades. A mode of conduct, a standard of courage, discipline, fortitude and integrity can do a great deal to make a woman beautiful.

—JACQUELINE BISSET

The most difficult thing in the world is to start a career known only for your looks, and then to try to become a serious actress. No one will take you seriously once you are known as the pretty woman.

—PENÉLOPE CRUZ

Being called gorgeous is not a bad thing! But at the same time,
I don't want to thrive on people's opinions of me.

—Lupita Nyong'o

～ဢ～

Because too much of my life was spent waiting to be seen.
Hoping to be seen, hoping to be picked. Once you realize that you
aren't looked at that way any more, other things start to happen
and you have to depend on other things to get by.

—Diane Keaton

～ဢ～

I always felt like my value was much more in my intellect than it
was in my appearance.

—Kerry Washington

～ဢ～

Women have face-lifts in a society in which women without
them appear to vanish from sight.

—Naomi Wolf

～ဢ～

There are some implausible standards out there.
It's really sad when I spend time with girls who are
11 years old and think they're fat.

—Jennifer Connelly

The psychic scars caused by believing you are ugly have a
permanent mark on your personality.

—JOAN RIVERS

⁓ ∿ ⁓

There's nothing moral about beauty.

—NADINE GORDIMER

⁓ ∿ ⁓

I think your whole life shows in your face
and you should be proud of that.

—LAUREN BACALL

⁓ ∿ ⁓

Ava Gardner was the most beautiful woman in the world, and it's
wonderful that she didn't cut up her face. She addressed aging by
picking up her chin and receiving the light in a better way.
And she looked like a woman. She never tried to look like a girl.

—SHARON STONE

⁓ ∿ ⁓

There should be more diversity. There are all different kinds of
beauty in the world. I mean, why aren't mothers glorified?
Instead, sex goddesses are glorified!

—JENNIFER CONNELLY

THE ART OF COMMUNICATION

Good communication is as stimulating
as black coffee, and just as hard
to sleep after.

—ANNE MORROW LINDBERGH

～∾～

My mother always taught us that if
people don't agree with you, the important
thing is to listen to them. But if you've
listened to them carefully and you still
think that you're right, then you must have
the courage of your convictions.

—JANE GOODALL

We are stronger when we listen, and smarter when we share.
—RANIA AL-ABDULLAH

⌐∞⌐

The opposite of talking is not listening.
The opposite of talking is waiting.
—FRAN LEBOWITZ

⌐∞⌐

Don't talk over me, don't argue with me, just listen.
—LAURA SCHLESSINGER

⌐∞⌐

I'll not listen to reason. Reason always means what
some one else has got to say.
—ELIZABETH GASKELL

⌐∞⌐

When we speak we are afraid our words will not be heard or
welcomed. But when we are silent, we are still afraid.
So it is better to speak.
—AUDRE LORDE

⌐∞⌐

Many times in life I've regretted the things I've said without
thinking. But I've never regretted the things I said nearly as much
as the words I left unspoken.
—LISA KLEYPAS

Blessed is the man who, having nothing to say, abstains from giving us wordy evidence of the fact.
—GEORGE ELIOT

~⌁~

Most conversations are simply monologues delivered in the presence of witnesses.
—MARGARET MILLAR

~⌁~

Polite conversation is rarely either.
—FRAN LEBOWITZ

~⌁~

Television has proved that people will look at anything rather than each other.
—ANN LANDERS

~⌁~

If you haven't got anything nice to say about anybody, come sit next to me.
—ALICE ROOSEVELT LONGWORTH

~⌁~

Don't say anything online that you wouldn't want plastered on a billboard with your face on it.
—ERIN BURY

I just believed. I believed that the technology would change people's lives. I believed putting real identity online—putting technology behind real identity—was the missing link.

—SHERYL SANDBERG

What is interesting is the power and the impact of social media....So we must try to use social media in a good way.

—MALALA YOUSAFZAI

I actually have this fantasy of giving up my cell phone.

—JULIA STILES

Everything we say signifies; everything counts, that we put out into the world. It impacts on kids, it impacts on the zeitgeist of the time.

—MERYL STREEP

I found I could say things with colors that I couldn't say in any other way—things that I had no words for.

—GEORGIA O'KEEFFE

The ability of writers to imagine what is not the self, to familiarize the strange and mystify the familiar, is the test of their power.

—TONI MORRISON

To know how to say what others only know how to think is what makes men poets or sages; and to dare to say what others only dare to think makes men martyrs or reformers or both.

—ELIZABETH CHARLES

I think that education is power. I think that being able to communicate with people is power. One of my main goals on the planet is to encourage people to empower themselves.

—OPRAH WINFREY

The body says what words cannot.

—MARTHA GRAHAM

WOMEN AND MEN

One is not born a woman:
one becomes one.
—SIMONE DE BEAUVOIR

~

In societies where men are truly confident
of their own worth, women are not
merely tolerated but valued.
—AUNG SAN SUU KYI

Men often say that women change their minds too much. I say they sometimes don't change them enough. I mean changing their state of mind, their attitudes, their outlook, their expectations, their consciousness—most of all, about themselves and what is possible in their lives.

—JULIA ALVAREZ

The especial genius of women I believe to be electrical in movement, intuitive in function, spiritual in tendency.

—MARGARET FULLER

Social science affirms that a woman's place in society marks the level of civilization.

—ELIZABETH CADY STANTON

Men have always been afraid that women could get along without them.

—MARGARET MEAD

I've got a woman's ability to stick to a job and get on with it when everyone else walks off and leaves it.

—MARGARET THATCHER

Toughness doesn't have to come in a pinstripe suit.

—Dianne Feinstein

I say if I'm beautiful. I say if I'm strong.
You will not determine my story—I will.

—Amy Schumer

Among poor people, there's not any question about women being strong—even stronger than men—they work in the fields right along with the men. When your survival is at stake, you don't have these questions about yourself like middle-class women do.

—Dolores Huerta

I hate to hear you talk about all women as if they were fine ladies instead of rational creatures. None of us want to be in calm waters all our lives.

—Jane Austen

Whether women are better than men I cannot say—
but I can say they are certainly no worse.

—Golda Meir

After all, Ginger Rogers did everything that Fred Astaire did. She just did it backward and in high heels.

—Ann Richards

❧

Men have had every advantage of us in telling their own story. Education has been theirs in so much higher a degree; the pen has been in their hands.

—Jane Austen

❧

Women are systematically degraded by receiving the trivial attentions which men think it manly to pay to the sex, when, in fact, men are insultingly supporting their own superiority.

—Mary Wollstonecraft

❧

Women who set a low value on themselves make life hard for all women.

—Nellie McClung

❧

I'd much rather be a woman than a man. Women can cry, they can wear cute clothes, and they're the first to be rescued off sinking ships.

—Gilda Radner

I love being a woman and I was not one of these women who rose through professional life by wearing men's clothes or looking masculine. I loved wearing bright colors and being who I am.

—Madeleine Albright

~⚬~

If men ever discovered how tough women actually are, they would be scared to death.

—Edna Ferber

~⚬~

I have the heart of a man, not a woman, and I am not afraid of anything.

—Elizabeth I

~⚬~

I do not wish women to have power over men; but over themselves.

—Mary Shelley

~⚬~

I am a woman meant for a man, but I never found a man who could compete.

—Bette Davis

Sometimes I wonder if men and women really suit each other.
Perhaps they should live next door and just visit now and then.
—KATHARINE HEPBURN

~∞~

I learned that women were smart and capable,
could live in community together without men,
and in fact did not need men much.
—ANNA QUINDLEN, ABOUT HER EXPERIENCE IN CATHOLIC SCHOOL

~∞~

We've begun to raise daughters more like sons...but few have
the courage to raise our sons more like our daughters.
—GLORIA STEINEM

~∞~

What is most beautiful in virile men is something feminine;
what is most beautiful in feminine women is something masculine.
—SUSAN SONTAG

SPIRITUALITY, MORALITY, AND VIRTUE

From the moment a soul has the grace to know God, she must seek.

—MOTHER TERESA

⁓

The essential thing to know about God is that God is Good. All the rest is secondary.

—SIMONE WEIL

God has always been to me not so much like a father as like
a dear and tender mother.

—HARRIET BEECHER STOWE

I believe that God is in me as the sun is in the color and fragrance
of a flower—the Light in my darkness, the Voice in my silence.

—HELEN KELLER

I happen to be a Christian, but I know that there is one God.
People worshipping goodness and love and kindness and truth are
worshipping the same God.

—ANNE LAMOTT

For prayer is the language of the heart—needing no measured
voice, no spoken tone.

—GRACE AGUILAR

Prayer is not asking. Prayer is putting oneself in the hands of
God, at his disposition, and listening to his voice
in the depths of our hearts.

—MOTHER TERESA

Learn to get in touch with the silence within yourself and know
that everything in this life has a purpose.
—Elisabeth Kubler-Ross

⟿

Intuition is a spiritual faculty, and does not explain,
but simply points the way.
—Florence Scovel Shinn

⟿

Meditation is the ultimate mobile device; you can use it
anywhere, anytime, unobtrusively.
—Sharon Salzberg

⟿

If women were convinced that a day off or an hour of solitude was
a reasonable ambition, they would find a way of attaining it.
As it is, they feel so unjustified in their demand that they rarely
make the attempt.
—Anne Morrow Lindbergh

⟿

The liar leads an existence of unutterable loneliness.
—Adrienne Rich

Grace fills empty spaces, but it can only enter where there is a voice to receive it, and it is grace itself which makes this void.

—SIMONE WEIL

Beauty and grace are performed whether or not we sense them. The least we can do is try to be there.

—ANNIE DILLARD

One thing that I ask of you: Never be afraid of giving. There is a deep joy in giving, since what we receive is much more that what we give.

—MOTHER TERESA

If you're going to care about the fall of the sparrow you can't pick and choose who's going to be the sparrow. It's everybody.

—MADELEINE L'ENGLE

Sometimes when we are generous in small, barely detectable ways it can change someone else's life forever.

—MARGARET CHO

This world is not conclusion.
A sequel stands beyond—
Invisible, as music—
But positive, as sound.

—Emily Dickinson

∽

I believe in the immortality of the soul because I have within me
immortal longings.

—Helen Keller

∽

The real things haven't changed. It is still best to be honest and
truthful; to make the most of what we have; to be happy with
simple pleasures; and have courage when things go wrong.

—Laura Ingalls Wilder

∽

Standing for right when it is unpopular is a true test
of moral character.

—Margaret Chase Smith

Simple, genuine goodness is the best capital to found the business of this life upon. It lasts when fame and money fail, and is the only riches we can take out of this world with us.

—LOUISA MAY ALCOTT

Being considerate of others will take you and your children further in life than any college or professional degree.

—MARIAN WRIGHT EDELMAN

The real test of class is how you treat people who cannot possibly do you any good.

—ANN LANDERS

The one thing that doesn't abide by majority rule is a person's conscience.

—HARPER LEE

As a family, we had a code, which was to do the right thing, do it the best we could, never complain and never take advantage.

—MARGARET TRUMAN

Parents can only give good advice or put them on the right paths,
but the final forming of a person's character lies in their own hands.

—ANNE FRANK

⟿

Our deeds still travel with us from afar,
And what we have been makes us what we are.

—GEORGE ELIOT

⟿

Nothing comes of so many things, if you have patience.

—JOYCE CAROL OATES

⟿

Humility must always being doing its work like a bee making its
honey in the hive: without humility all will be lost.

—ST. TERESA OF AVILA

⟿

The truth needs so little rehearsal.

—BARBARA KINGSOLVER

When hope is taken away from the people,
moral degeneration follows swiftly after.
—Pearl S. Buck

~∞~

To give without any reward, or any notice,
has a special quality of its own.
—Anne Morrow Lindbergh

~∞~

Not all of us can do great things.
But we can small things with great love.
—Mother Teresa

POVERTY
AND RICHES

To live in poverty is to live with constant
uncertainty, to accept galling indignities,
and to expect harassment by the police,
welfare officials, and employers, as well as
by others who are poor and desperate.

—BARBARA EHRENREICH

~⚬~

Hungry people cannot be good at
learning or producing anything, except
perhaps violence.

—PEARL BAILEY

Until we end the masculinization of wealth,
we will not end the feminization of poverty.

—GLORIA STEINEM

～✺～

Poverty is sexist. Women and girls are more likely to be
impoverished, less likely to get an education and more likely to
suffer bad health. And when they're born into poverty, it's much
more difficult for them to lift themselves and their families out of
it. Why? One reason is that breaking out of poverty takes time—
and that's a resource women around the world are short on.

—MELINDA GATES

～✺～

The economic dependence of women is perhaps the greatest
injustice that has been done to us, and has worked the greatest
injury to the race.

—NELLIE MCCLUNG

～✺～

Poverty is not about color.

—QUEEN LATIFAH

～✺～

Money helps, though not so much as you think when
you don't have it.

—LOUISE ERDRICH

The greatest thing I ever was able to do was give a welfare
check back.

—Whoopi Goldberg

~

The only way not to think of money is to have a great deal of it.

—Edith Wharton

~

I've been rich and I've been poor. Believe me, honey, rich is better.

—Sophie Tucker

~

Economy was always "elegant," and money-spending always
"vulgar" and ostentatious—a sort of sour-grapeism, which made
us very peaceful and satisfied.

—Elizabeth Gaskell

~

I don't know much about being a millionaire,
but I'll bet I'd be darling at it.

—Dorothy Parker

~

Perhaps too much of everything is as bad as too little.

—Edna Ferber

I'd rather have roses on my table, than diamonds on my neck.

—EMMA GOLDMAN

～○～

I never hated a man enough to give him diamonds back.

—ZSA ZSA GABOR

～○～

I truly believe that women should be financially independent from their men. And let's face it, money gives men the power to run the show. It gives men the power to define value. They define what's sexy. And men define what's feminine. It's ridiculous.

—BEYONCÉ

～○～

It is easy to be independent when you've got money. But to be independent when you haven't got a thing, that's the Lord's test.

—MAHALIA JACKSON

～○～

The easiest way for your children to learn about money is for you not to have any.

—KATHERINE WHITEHORN

～○～

It is more rewarding to watch money change the world than watch it accumulate.

—GLORIA STEINEM

YESTERDAY, TODAY, AND TOMORROW

One faces the future with one's past.
—PEARL S. BUCK

~∞~

Anyone who limits her vision to memories of yesterday is already dead.
—LILY LANGTRY

We inhabit ourselves without valuing ourselves, unable to see that here, now, this very moment is sacred; but once it's gone—its value is incontestable.

—JOYCE CAROL OATES

⁓

It is terribly amusing how many different climates of feeling one can go through in a day.

—ANNE MORROW LINDBERGH

⁓

You had better live your best and act your best and think your best today; for today is the sure preparation for tomorrow and all the other tomorrows that follow.

—HARRIET MARTINEAU

⁓

Today the problem that has no name, is how to juggle work, love, home and children.

—BETTY FRIEDAN

⁓

It's not perfect, but to me on balance Right Now is a lot better than the Good Old Days.

—MAEVE BINCHY

There are years that ask questions and years that answer.
—ZORA NEALE HURSTON

You need only claim the events of your life to make yourself yours.
When you truly possess all you have been and done, which may
take some time, you are fierce with reality.
—FLORIDA SCOTT-MAXWELL

The future depends entirely on what each of us does every day.
—GLORIA STEINEM

The future belongs to those who believe
in the beauty of their dreams.
—ELEANOR ROOSEVELT

Women may be the one group that grows more radical with age.
—GLORIA STEINEM

Old age is like a plane flying through a storm. Once you are
aboard there is nothing you can do.
—GOLDA MEIR

Surely the consolation prize of age is in finding out how few
things are worth worrying over, and how many things that we once
desired, we don't want anymore.

—DOROTHY DIX

⁓

One does not get better but different and older
and that is always a pleasure.

—GERTRUDE STEIN

⁓

What I don't understand is this assumption that aging means
isolation. There's just so much to do in the world—so many people
who need an ally, so many children who need hugging. I refuse to
believe being elderly and being lonely go hand in hand.

—DIANE SAWYER

⁓

I have always felt that a woman had the right to treat the subject
of her age with ambiguity until, perhaps, she passed into the realm
of over ninety. Then it is better she be candid with herself
and with the world.

—HELENA RUBENSTEIN

⁓

For years I wanted to be older, and now I am.

—MARGARET ATWOOD

The years seem to rush by now, and I think of death as a fast approaching end of a journey—double and treble reason for loving as well as working while it is day.

—George Eliot

~

At the end of your life you will never regret not having passed one more test, winning one more verdict or not closing one more deal. You will regret time not spent with a husband, a child, a friend or a parent.

—Barbara Bush

~

You don't get to choose how you're going to die. Or when. You can decide how you're going to live now.

—Joan Baez

THE WORLD AROUND US

No country can ever truly flourish if
it stifles the potential of its women and
deprives itself of the contributions of
half its citizens.
—MICHELLE OBAMA

Mankind will endure when the world
appreciates the logic of diversity.
—INDIRA GANDHI

I had gone from believing that women's issues were a distraction... to the realization that women are the issue, the core issue. We will fail to solve any problem—poverty, peace, sustainable development, environment, health—unless we look at it through a gender lens and make sure the solution will be good for women.

—JANE FONDA

~

The worst thing that we can do as women is not stand up for each other, and this is something we can practice every day, no matter where we are and what we do—women sticking up for other women, choosing to protect and celebrate each other instead of competing or criticizing one another.

—AMAL CLOONEY

~

Let us develop respect for all living things. Let us try to replace violence and intolerance with understanding and compassion. And love.

—JANE GOODALL

~

Every aspect of our lives is, in a sense, a vote for the kind of world we want to live in.

—FRANCES MOORE LAPPÉ

One individual cannot possibly make a difference, alone. It is individual efforts, collectively, that makes a noticeable difference— all the difference in the world!

—JANE GOODALL

～

We have forgotten how to be good guests, how to walk lightly on the earth as its other creatures do.

—BARBARA WARD

～

We won't have a society if we destroy the environment.

—MARGARET MEAD

～

Those who contemplate the beauty of the earth find reserves of strength that will endure as long as life lasts.

—RACHEL CARSON

～

Never doubt that a small number of dedicated people can change the world; indeed it is the only thing that ever has.

—MARGARET MEAD

Wisdom and Inspiration

Without leaps of imagination or dreaming, we lose the excitement of possibilities. Dreaming, after all, is a form of planning.

—Gloria Steinem

—◦—

I'm obsessive about imagination and the link from imagination to the sense of possibility.

—Maxine Greene

Figuring out who you are is the whole point of
the human experience.

—ANNA QUINDLEN

⁓

Our deepest wishes are whispers of our authentic selves.
We must learn to respect them. We must learn to listen.

—SARAH BAN BREATHNACH

⁓

One of the lessons that I grew up with was to always stay true to
yourself and never let what somebody else says distract you from
your goals. And so when I hear about negative and false attacks,
I really don't invest any energy in them, because I know who I am.

—MICHELLE OBAMA

⁓

I think the key is for women not to set any limits.

—MARTINA NAVRATILOVA

⁓

I think when we experience emotion we should delve into it and
live through it. We are always trying to shut off pain or control our
happiness. Why? To live is to feel.

—GWYNETH PALTROW

I don't think of all the misery, but of the beauty that still remains.

—Anne Frank

~

We often take for granted the very things that most
deserve our gratitude.

—Cynthia Ozick

~

Our way is not soft grass, it's a mountain path with lots of rocks.
But it goes upwards, forward, toward the sun.

—Ruth Westheimer

~

No pessimist ever discovered the secrets of the stars, or sailed to
an uncharted land, or opened a new heaven to the human spirit.

—Helen Keller

~

If you can't change your fate, change your attitude.

—Amy Tan

~

What people in the world think of you is really none
of your business.

—Martha Graham

Being powerful is like being a lady. If you have to
tell people you are, you aren't.

—MARGARET THATCHER

The most common way people give up their power is
by thinking they don't have any.

—ALICE WALKER

I don't need a man to rectify my existence.
The most profound relationship we'll ever have is
the one with ourselves.

—SHIRLEY MACLAINE

Measure not the work until the day's out and the labor done.

—ELIZABETH BARRETT BROWNING

Surround yourself with only people who are
going to lift you higher.

—OPRAH WINFREY

You can't do it alone. As you navigate through the rest of your life, be open to collaboration. Other people and other people's ideas are often better than your own. Find a group of people who challenge and inspire you, spend a lot of time with them, and it will change your life.

—Amy Poehler

Women have to summon up courage to fulfill dormant dreams.

—Alice Walker

Imagine that we conjure up a world that is safe for mothers and daughters.

—Louise Bernikow

I so believe that older women have tremendous value to their families, their community, their country, their world.

—Sally Field

As women, we must stand up for each other.

—Michelle Obama

What do we live for, if it is not to make life
less difficult for each other?
—George Eliot

～⌒～

Don't compromise yourself. You are all you've got.
—Janis Joplin

～⌒～

Follow what you are genuinely passionate about and let that
guide you to your destination.
—Diane Sawyer

～⌒～

Life was meant to be lived, and curiosity must be kept alive. One
must never, for whatever reason, turn one's back on life.
—Eleanor Roosevelt

～⌒～

Say no when you don't want to do something.
Say yes if your instincts are strong,
even if everyone around you disagrees.
Decide whether you want to be liked or admired.
Decide if fitting in is more important than finding
out what you're doing here.
Believe in kissing.
—Eve Ensler

Exhaust the little moment. Soon it dies.
And be it gash or gold it will not come
Again in this identical disguise.

—GWENDOLYN BROOKS

How we spend our days is, of course, how we spend our lives.

—ANNIE DILLARD

Stay afraid, but do it anyway.
What's important is the action.
You don't have to wait to be confident.
Just do it and eventually the confidence will follow.

—CARRIE FISHER

Don't let anyone rob you of your imagination,
your creativity,
or your curiosity.

—MAE JEMISON

CONTRIBUTORS

BELLA ABZUG (1920–1998) — American politician

ABIGAIL ADAMS (1744–1818) — Writer and First Lady of the United States

CHIMAMANDA NGOZI ADICHIE (b. 1977) — Nigerian writer and activist

GRACE AGUILAR (1816–1847) — English writer and theologian

RANIA AL-ABDULLAH (b. 1970) — Kuwait-born Queen of Jordan and wife of King Abullah II

MADELEINE ALBRIGHT (b. 1937) — Czech-born American politician and diplomat; U.S. Secretary of State

LOUISA MAY ALCOTT (1832–1888) — American novelist

ISABEL ALLENDE (b. 1942) — Chilean writer

JULIA ALVAREZ (b. 1950) — American writer

CHRISTIANE AMANPOUR (b. 1958) — British-Iranian journalist and television host

MARIAN ANDERSON (1897–1993) — American opera singer

SUSAN B. ANTHONY (1820–1906) — Pioneer in U.S. women's suffrage movement

HANNAH ARENDT (1906–1975) — German-born American political philosopher and writer

LADY NANCY ASTOR (1879–1964) — English Viscountess, MP in British House of Commons

Margaret Atwood (b. 1939) — Canadian writer and activist

Jane Austen (1775–1817) — English novelist

Lauren Bacall (1924–2014) — American actress and writer

Joan Baez (b. 1941) — American folksinger, songwriter, musician, and activist

Pearl Bailey (1918–1990) — American singer

Ella J. Baker (1903–1986) — American civil rights activist

Sarah Ban Breathnach (b. 1948) — English writer

Roseanne Barr (b. 1952) — American actress

Mary Catherine Bateson (b. 1939) — American writer and cultural anthropologist

Ingrid Bergman (1915–1982) — Swedish actress

Louise Berkinow (b. 1940) — American writer and activist

Halle Berry (b. 1966) — American actress and model

Maeve Binchy (1940–2012) — Irish writer

Jacqueline Bisset (b. 1944) — English actress

Elizabeth Blackwell (1821–1910) — American physician

Amy Bloom (b. 1953) — American writer

Emily Blunt (b. 1983) — British-American actress

Erma Bombeck (1927–1996) — American humorist and writer

Margaret Bonnano (b. 1950) — American writer

Barbara Boxer (b. 1940) — American politician

Anne Brontë (1820–1849) — English novelist and poet

Charlotte Brontë (1816–1855) — English novelist and poet

EMILY BRONTË (1818–1848) — English novelist and poet

GWENDOLYN BROOKS (1917–2000) — American poet

JOYCE BROTHERS (1925–1913) — American psychologist and writer

RITA MAE BROWN (b. 1944) — American writer and activist

ELIZABETH BARRETT BROWNING (1806–1861) — English poet

PEARL S. BUCK (1892–1973) — American novelist

GISELE BUNDCHEN (b. 1980) — Brazilian supermodel, businesswoman

ERIN BURY (b. 1986) — Canadian marketing executive, tech writer and speaker

BARBARA BUSH (b. 1925) — First Lady of the United States and humanitarian

RACHEL CARSON (1907–1964) — American marine biologist, conservationist, and writer

MARY CASSATT (1844–1926) — American painter

WILLA CATHER (1873–1947) — American novelist, poet, journalist, and editor

COCO CHANEL (1883–1971) — French fashion designer and businesswoman

ELIZABETH CHARLES (1828–1896) — English writer

JULIA CHILD (1912–2004) — American chef, writer, and television personality

LYDIA MARIA CHILD (1802–1880) — American activist and writer

SHIRLEY CHISHOLM (1924–2005) — American politician, educator, and writer

MARGARET CHO (b. 1968) — American comedian, writer, and actress

AGATHA CHRISTIE (1890–1976) — English writer

CHELSEA CLINTON (b. 1980) — American activist, journalist, and writer

HILLARY CLINTON (b. 1947) — American politician, former Secretary of State, former First Lady of the United States

AMAL CLOONEY (b. 1978) — Lebanese-British lawyer and activist

COLETTE (1873–1954) — French novelist and performer

JENNIFER CONNELLY (b. 1970) — American actress

LAVERNE COX (b. 1984) — American actress and LGBT activist

PENÉLOPE CRUZ (b. 1974) — Spanish actress and model

MARIE CURIE (1867–1934) — French-Polish physicist and chemist

BETTE DAVIS (1908–1991) — American actress

SIMONE DE BEAUVOIR (1908–1986) — French novelist and activist

ELLEN DEGENERES (b. 1958) — American comedian, writer, television host, and activist

AGNES DE MILLE (1881–1959) — American choreographer, dancer, and writer

ANITA DIAMANT (b. 1951) —American writer

MARIAN C. DIAMOND (b. 1926) — American academic and founder of modern neuroscience

EMILY DICKINSON (1830–1886) — American poet

MARLENE DIETRICH (1901–1992) — German-born actress and singer .

ANI DIFRANCO (b. 1970) — American singer-songwriter and musician

ANNIE DILLARD (b. 1945) — American writer and professor

DOROTHY DIX (1861–1951) — American journalist

MAUREEN DOWD (b. 1952) — American journalist and writer

COLETTE DOWLING (b. 1938) — American psychotherapist and writer

ISADORA DUNCAN (1877–1927) — American dancer

AMELIA EARHART (1897–1937?) — American aviator and writer

MARIAN WRIGHT EDELMAN (b. 1939) —American children's rights
   activist

BARBARA EHRENREICH (b. 1941) — American writer and activist

GEORGE ELIOT (1819–1880) — English novelist

ELIZABETH I (1533–1603) — British monarch

EVE ENSLER (b. 1953) — American writer, performer, and activist

LOUISE ERDRICH (b. 1954) — American writer

DIANNE FEINSTEIN (b. 1933) — American politician

EDNA FERBER (1887–1968) — American novelist and playwright

GERALDINE A. FERRARO (1935–2011) — American lawyer and politician

TINA FEY (b. 1970) — American actress, writer, comedian, and producer

CARRIE FISHER (1956–2016) — American actress, writer, and mental
   health advocate

JANE FONDA (b. 1937) — American actress, writer, activist, and fitness
   expert

BETTY FORD (1918–2011) — First Lady of the United States, co-founder
   of The Betty Ford Center

JODIE FOSTER (b. 1962) — American actress, director, and producer

ANNE FRANK (1929–1945) — German diarist

JUDITH FREEMAN (b. 1946) — American writer

MARILYN FRENCH (1929–2009) — American writer

BETTY FRIEDAN (1921–2006) — American writer and activist

MARGARET FULLER (1810–1850) — American journalist and critic

ZSA ZSA GABOR (b. 1917) — Hungarian-born American actress and socialite

INDIRA GANDHI (1917–1984) — prime minister of India

ELISABETH GASKELL (1810–1865) — English writer

MELINDA GATES (b. 1964) — American businesswoman and philanthropist

ROXANE GAY (b. 1974) — American writer, professor, and commentator

ELIZABETH GILBERT (b. 1969) — American writer

CHARLOTTE PERKINS GILMAN (1860–1935) — American writer and lecturer

RUTH BADER GINSBURG (b. 1933) — U.S. Supreme Court Justice

WHOOPI GOLDBERG (b. 1955) — American actress, comedian, activist, writer, and talk-show host

EMMA GOLDMAN (1869–1940) — Russian-born American writer, anarchist, and activist

JANE GOODALL (b. 1934) — English primatologist, ethologist, anthropologist, and activist

DORIS KEARNS GOODWIN (b. 1943) — American biographer, historian, and political commentator

NADINE GORDIMER (1923–2014) — South African writer and political activist

KATHARINE GRAHAM (1917–2001) — American newspaper publisher

MARTHA GRAHAM (1899–1991) — American dancer and choreographer

MAXINE GREENE (1917–2014) — American education philosopher, writer, teacher, and activist

GERMAINE GREER (b. 1939) — Australian writer and activist

MIA HAMM (b. 1972) — American professional soccer player (retired) and writer

MARY HARNEY (b. 1953) — Irish politician

JULIE HARRIS (1925–2013) — American actress

LOUISE HART (b. 19??) — American psychologist, writer, and speaker

KATHARINE HEPBURN (1907–2003) — American actress

BELL HOOKS (b. 1952) — American writer and activist

GRACE HOPPER (1906–1992) — American military and computer scientist

LENA HORNE (1917–2010) — American singer, actress, dancer, and activist

JULIA WARD HOWE (1819–1910) — American abolitionist, activist, and writer

DOLORES HUERTA (b. 1930) — American labor leader and activist

ZORA NEALE HURSTON (1891–1960) — American writer, folklorist, and anthropologist

MAHALIA JACKSON (1911–1972) — American Gospel singer

MAE JEMISON (b. 1956) — American physicist and astronaut

SARAH ORNE JEWETT (1849–1909) —American novelist and short-story writer

ANGELINA JOLIE (b. 1975) — American actress, writer, director, and humanitarian

MOTHER JONES (1830–1930) — Irish-American labor organizer and humanitarian, a.k.a. Mary Harris Jones

JANIS JOPLIN (1943-1970) — American singer-songwriter

MINDY KALING (b. 1979) — American actress, writer, producer, and director

MARY KARR (b. 1955) — American poet, writer, and professor

DIANE KEATON (b. 1946) — American actress director, producer, and screenwriter

HELEN KELLER (1880–1968) — American writer, activist, and educator

CAROLINE KENNEDY (b. 1957) — American writer, attorney, and U.S. ambassador

CORETTA SCOTT KING (1927–2006) — American activist and wife of Dr. Martin Luther King, Jr.

BARBARA KINGSOLVER (b. 1955) — American writer

LISA KLEYPAS (b. 1964) — American writer

KEIRA KNIGHTLEY (b. 1985) — English actress

BEYONCÉ KNOWLES-CARTER (b. 1981) — American singer/songwriter and actress

ELIZABETH KÜBLER-ROSS (1926–2004) — Swiss-American psychiatrist and writer

LADY GAGA (b. 1986) — American singer-songwriter and actress; born Stefani Germanotta

HEDY LAMARR (1913–2000) — Austro-American actress and inventor

MARY LAMB (1764–1847) — English writer

ANNE LAMOTT (b. 1954) — American novelist and non-fiction writer

ANN LANDERS (1918–2002) — American advice columnist and talk-show host

LILY LANGTRY (1853–1929) — English actor

FRANCES MOORE LAPPÉ (b. 1944) — American writer and activist

QUEEN LATIFA (b. 1970) — American singer/songwriter, rap artist, model, and actress; born Dana Elaine Owens

SARA LAWRENCE-LIGHTFOOT (b. 1944) — American sociologist

FRAN LEBOWITZ (b. 1950) — American writer and social critic

HARPER LEE (1926–2016) — American writer

MADELEINE L'ENGLE (1918–2007) — American writer

DORIS LESSING (1919–2013) — English writer

MAYA LIN (b. 1959) — American architectural designer and artist

ANNE MORROW LINDBERGH (1906–2001) — American writer and aviator

CHRIS EVERT LLOYD (b. 1954) — American professional tennis player

ALICE ROOSEVELT LONGWORTH (1884–1980) — American socialite, political wit, and eldest daughter of Theodore Roosevelt

AUDRE LORDE (1934–1992) — American writer and activist

CLARE BOOTH LUCE (1903–1987) — American writer and diplomat

SHIRLEY MACLAINE (b. 1934) — American actress, dancer, and writer

MADONNA (b. 1958) — American singer/songwriter, actress, and activist; born Madonna Ciccone

WILMA PEARL MANKILLER (1945–2010) — Native American activist, first female Chief of the Cherokee Nation

HARRIET MARTINEAU (1802–1876) — English novelist, journalist, economic and historical writer

MARY MCALEESE (b. 1951) — Irish politician

MIGNON MCLAUGHLIN (1913–1983) — American journalist and writer

NELLIE MCLUNG (1873–1951) — Canadian politician and activist

MARGARET MEAD (1901–1978) — American cultural-anthropologist and writer

GOLDA MEIR (1898–1978) — Founder of the State of Israel and fourth Prime Minister of Israel

ANGELA MERKEL (b. 1954) — German politician and Chancellor of Germany

ALICE MEYNELL (1847–1922) — English writer and activist

BETTE MIDLER (b. 1945) — American actress, singer/songwriter, and comedian

MARGARET MILLAR (1915–1994) — American-Canadian writer

HELEN MIRREN (b. 1945) — English actress

NANCY MITFORD (1904–1973) — English writer and journalist

MARILYN MONROE (1926–1962) — American actress, model, and singer

TONI MORRISON (b. 1931) — American novelist, editor, and professor

ALICE MUNRO (b. 1931) — Canadian writer

IRIS MURDOCH (1919–1999) — Irish-born English writer and philosopher

MARTINA NAVRATILOVA (b. 1956) — Czech-born American tennis player and coach

FLORENCE NIGHTINGALE (1820–1910) — English nurse, founder, and social activist

ANAIS NÏN (1903–1977) — French-born American writer

KATHLEEN NORRIS (b. 1947) — American poet and essayist

LUPITA NYONG'O (b. 1983) — Mexican-Kenyan actress

FLANNERY O'CONNOR (1925–1964) — American writer

GEORGIA O'KEEFFE (1887–1986) — American painter

JANE O'REILLY (b. 1936) — American writer and activist

JOYCE CAROL OATES (b. 1938) — American writer

MICHELLE OBAMA (b. 1964) — lawyer, writer, former First Lady of the United States, humanitarian

JACQUELINE KENNEDY ONASSIS (1929–1994) — First Lady of the United States, activist, editor

CYNTHIA OZICK (b. 1928) — American novelist, essayist, and short-story writer

CAMILLE PAGLIA (b. 1947) — American writer, academic, and social critic

GWYNETH PALTROW (b. 1972) — American actress, singer, writer,

EMMELINE PANKHURST (1858–1928) — English activist

DOROTHY PARKER (1893–1967) — American writer and poet

ROSA PARKS (1913–2005) — American civil rights activist

ANNA PAVLOVA (1881–1931) — Russian ballerina

MARY PICKFORD (1892–1979) — Canadian actress and film studio co-founder

BELVA PLAIN (1915–2010) — American writer

AMY POEHLER (b. 1971) — American actress, comedian, writer, director, and producer

NATALIE PORTMAN (b. 1981) — American actress

ANNA QUINDLEN (b. 1952) — American writer, novelist, and journalist

GILDA RADNER (1946–1989) — American comedian and actress

JEANETTE RANKIN (1880–1973) — American politician

CONDOLEEZZA RICE (b. 1954) — American political scientist, diplomat, U.S. Secretary of State

ADRIENNE RICH (1929–2012) — American poet, essayist, and activist

ANN RICHARDS (1933–2006) — American politician

JOAN RIVERS (1933–2014) — American comedian, writer, actress, and television personality

ELEANOR ROOSEVELT (1884–1962) — American humanitarian, political activist, and longest-serving First Lady of the United States

J. K. ROWLING (b. 1965) — English novelist

HELENA RUBENSTEIN (1870–1965) — Polish-born American entrepreneur

RITA RUDNER (b. 1953) — American comedian, writer, and actress

SHARON SALZBERG (b. 1952) — American writer and teacher of Buddhism

AUNG SAN SUU KYI (b. 1945) — Burmese political leader

GEORGE SAND (1804–1876) — French writer

SHERYL SANDBERG (b. 1969) — American business executive and writer

MAY SARTON (1912–1995) — American writer

DIANE SAWYER (b. 1945) — American broadcast journalist

LAURA SCHLESSINGER (b. 1947) — American writer and commentator

AMY SCHUMER (b. 1981) — American comedian, writer, actress, and producer

FLORIDA SCOTT-MAXWELL (1883–1979) — American writer and psychologist

ST. ELIZABETH ANN SETON (1774–1821) — Educator, Roman Catholic nun, and first American saint

SHAKIRA (b. 1977) — Columbian singer/songwriter; born Shakira Ripoli

GAIL SHEEHY (b. 1937) — American writer, journalist, and lecturer

FLORENCE SCOVEL SHINN (1871–1940) — American artist and writer

MARGARET CHASE SMITH (1897–1995) — American politician

PATTI SMITH (b. 1946) — American poet, singer/songwriter

ZADIE SMITH (b. 1975) — English novelist, essayist, and short-story writer

SUSAN SONTAG (1933–2004) — American writer, filmmaker, professor, and political activist

SONIA SOTOMAYOR (b. 1954) — U.S. Supreme Court Justice

ELIZABETH CADY STANTON (1815–1902) — American social activist, abolitionist, and a pioneer of the women's rights movement

GERTRUDE STEIN (1874–1946) — American writer

GLORIA STEINEM (b. 1936) — American writer, journalist, political and social activist

JULIA STILES (b. 1981) — American actress

ELIZABETH STONE (b. 19??) — American writer and professor

SHARON STONE (b. 1958) — American actress, producer, and former model

HARRIET BEECHER STOWE (1811–1896) — American writer and abolitionist

MERYL STREEP (b. 1949) — American actress

BARBRA STREISAND (b. 1942) — American singer/songwriter, writer, actress, film producer, and director

ANNE SULLIVAN (1866–1936) — American educator

AMY TAN (b. 1952) — American writer

ELIZABETH TAYLOR (1932–2011) — British-born American actress and humanitarian

CORRIE TEN BOOM (1892–1983) — Dutch writer and activist

ST. TERESA OF AVILA (1515–1582) — Spanish mystic, Roman Catholic nun, and Roman Catholic saint

ST. TERESA OF CALCUTTA (Mother Teresa) (1910–1997) — Albanian-born Roman Catholic nun, canonized in 2016, who devoted her life to the poor of Calcutta

MARGARET THATCHER (1925–2013) — British politician and former Prime Minister of the United Kingdom

MARLO THOMAS (b. 1937) — American actress, producer, and activist

REBECCA TRAISTER (b. 1975) — American writer

MARGARET TRUMAN (1924–2008) —American singer, writer, and daughter of President Harry S. Truman

SOJOURNER TRUTH (1797–1883) — American abolitionist and activist

HARRIET TUBMAN (1820–1913) — American abolitionist and humanitarian

BARBARA TUCHMAN (1912–1989) — American writer and historian

SOPHIE TUCKER (1884–1966) — Russian-born American singer, actress, and comedian

CHRISTY TURLINGTON (b. 1969) — American supermodel

TINA TURNER (b. 1939) — American singer and actress

HARRIET VAN HORNE (1920–1998) —American journalist and critic

GLORIA VANDERBILT (b. 1924) — American artist, writer, heiress, and entrepreneur

SUZANNE VEGA (b. 1959) — American singer-songwriter

QUEEN VICTORIA (1819–1901) — British monarch

DIANE VON FURSTENBERG (b. 1946) — Belgium-born American designer

LILLIAN WALD (1867–1940) — American nurse, humanitarian, and writer

ALICE WALKER (b. 1944) — American novelist, poet, and activist

BARBARA WALTERS (b. 1931) — American broadcast journalist and writer

BARBARA WARD (1914–1981) — British economist and writer

ELIZABETH WARREN (b. 1949) — American academic and politician

KERRY WASHINGTON (b. 1977) — American actress

MARTHA WASHINGTON (1732–1802) — First Lady of the United States

WENDY WASSERSTEIN (1950–2006) — American playwright

EMMA WATSON (b. 1990) — British actress

FAYE WATTLETON (b. 1943) — American educator and activist

SIMONE WEIL (1909–1943) — French philosopher, Christian mystic, and activist

MAE WEST (1893–1980) — American actress, singer, screenwriter, and playwright

REBECCA WEST (1892–1983) — British journalist, literary critic, and writer

RUTH WESTHEIMER (b. 1928) — German-born American sex therapist, writer, and media personality

EDITH WHARTON (1862–1937) — American novelist

KATHERINE WHITEHORN (b. 1928) — British journalist and writer

LAURA INGALLS WILDER (1867–1957) American writer

OPRAH WINFREY (b. 1954) — American media mogul, talk-show host, actress, and philanthropist

DEBRA WINGER (b. 1955) — American actress

NAOMI WOLF (b. 1962) — American writer and activist

MARY WOLLSTONECRAFT (1759–1797) — English writer, philosopher, and activist

JOANNE WOODWARD (b. 1930) — American actress

Virginia Woolf (1892–1941) — English writer

Chien-Shiung Wu (1912–1997) — Chinese-American experimental physicist

Rosalyn Yalow (1921–2011) — American medical physicist

Malala Yousafzai (b. 1997) — Pakistani activist and writer